THE 5-YEAR-OLD
CEO

the Power of Childlike Curiosity in Leadership

HUNTER McMAHON

LUCIDBOOKS

Dedication

For my kids, who never stopped asking questions and helped me understand the importance of lifelong curiosity.

Contents

Foreword...ix

Introduction...1

Chapter 1: The Curious Questioner 7

Chapter 2: The Listening Leader 15

Chapter 3: Challenging the Status Quo.......25

Chapter 4: All for One 35

Chapter 5: Calm in the Storm....................47

Chapter 6: Riding the Winds of Change 59

Chapter 7: Lifting Others..........................71

Conclusion..83

References 89

Special Thanks

To my wife: thank you for always supporting my musings, wild ideas, and dot-connecting tangents. Your belief in me (and patience) makes everything possible.

To my four amazing kids: thank you for keeping life endlessly curious with your nonstop questions, even before I've had coffee (a bold move, and yet . . . we've both survived). You inspire more of this book than you know.

To the clients and teammates at iDiscovery Solutions: thank you for the trust, collaboration, and challenges that have shaped my journey. The lessons I've learned alongside you helped frame every page of this book.

Foreword

I really got to know Hunter McMahon when a technology-based project we were working on went a bit off the rails. When I called to discuss the problem, I couldn't believe what I heard. Actually, it was what I didn't hear that stood out. No excuses, no finger-pointing, no nonsense. Instead, Hunter asked questions to identify the issues, their scope, and consequences. He listened, even when I got a little loud and certainly when I said things he didn't prefer to hear. We then collaborated on crafting a solution that earned my trust and respect. In a crisis, Hunter demonstrated leadership.

Now, when I need advice on leadership, Hunter is my first call. Driven by an endless desire to learn, he has always just read the latest book or listened to the latest podcast. I also call Hunter when the latest promises (or threats) about AI make me question what I think I know. But Hunter's a really smart guy, so sometimes I have to ask him to "Tell me like I'm 5." I guess I said that one too many times! In "The 5-Year-Old CEO: The Power of Child-like Curiosity in Leadership," Hunter reminds us all how to lead, even as the world changes rapidly around us. Ask questions. Truly listen to the answers. Ask more questions. Solve problems together. None of these concepts is revolutionary. But Hunter presents them in vignettes we have all lived and then illustrates them with examples from world and business leaders. These lessons are utterly relatable and so easily applied. In fact, they are so easy that even a five-year-old . . . well, you get the point.

—Daniel Plunkett
In-House Counsel,
Chair of Practice Groups,
Litigator, Husband and Father

Introduction

Imagine a boardroom where curiosity reigns, empathy flows, and even the toughest problems are met with childlike wonder. In a world increasingly driven by artificial intelligence and rapid change, our natural human strengths of curiosity, empathy, and creativity have become our most vital leadership assets. Yet, many leaders feel pressured to have all the answers, to project infallibility. This book offers a different perspective: what if the key to leading in an AI-driven world is to think a bit more like a five-year-old?

The 5-Year-Old CEO: The Power of Childlike Curiosity in Leadership is a journey through seven core leadership principles, each illuminated by the unlikeliest of mentors—a curious, compassionate five-year-old named Eric. Eric is not a prodigy or a CEO in miniature; he's a normal child who, in the course of everyday kindergarten adventures, demonstrates timeless truths about leadership. His stories are simple and relatable: resolving playground conflicts, asking questions in class, helping a friend learn. But within these humble classroom moments lie powerful lessons that echo through the halls of corporate offices, law firms, and tech start-ups alike.

Each chapter of this book follows a consistent and enriching pattern. We begin with one of Eric's stories, a series of fictional vignettes that set the stage by showing how a fundamental leadership trait can manifest in a child's world. These aren't fairy tales where Eric does everything perfectly; he stumbles, learns, and grows, just as we all do. Following each story, we delve into the adult leadership lesson at hand, exploring why it matters and how it applies to leading teams and organizations. Along the way, I've included real-world examples, drawn from business, history, or current events, to show how the principle plays out on the grand stage of adult life. These examples serve as a bridge, connecting the innocence of Eric's classroom to the complex reality of your workplace.

Finally, in each chapter, I will provide you with a reflective takeaway. These help distill the chapter's insights into practical wisdom you can carry with you. Think of them as your Monday-morning leadership pep talks, or words of encouragement to apply what you've learned as soon as you step into your office (or onto your next virtual meeting).

You may ask why I chose to frame a leadership book around the mindset of a five-year-old? Because in our early years, before experience and education teach us boundaries, we are naturally curious, boldly imaginative, and unafraid to express emotion. We ask "why" incessantly. We speak our minds honestly. We look at the world without cynicism.

Over time, many of us lose some of that openness. We build up assumptions, habits, and fears of looking foolish. Ironically, those childlike qualities are exactly what today's complex, fast-changing world demands of leaders. The most innovative companies seek leaders who are curious learners rather than those who claim to know it all. The most resilient teams flourish under leaders who listen and care, rather than command and control.

Through this book, I invite you to reclaim and sharpen those essential leadership qualities you once practiced as a child. Whether you're a senior partner at a law firm navigating industry disruption, an executive at a tech company driving AI integration, or a manager at a professional services firm leading a diverse team through change, these lessons will resonate. They'll remind you that effective leadership isn't about age, title, or knowing the "right" answers. It's about asking better questions, connecting with people, challenging the status quo, working together, resolving differences, adapting with grace, and lifting others up.

As you read, you'll find that each chapter stands on its own with a specific focus, but together they form a holistic picture of adaptive, human-centered leadership. From embracing curiosity to becoming a mentor, the journey will equip you with insights and stories to reflect on your own leadership style. Take your time with them. Reflect on Eric's classroom and how its lessons might apply to your conference room. Leadership growth is a continuous process, much like a child growing and learning day by day.

Ultimately, *The 5-Year-Old- CEO* is about the power of rediscovering fundamental human strengths in a technologically advanced world. It's about leading with questions and compassion at a time when answers are cheap, but understanding is priceless. And it's about the quiet confidence that comes from knowing that sometimes the best leadership wisdom comes not from advanced degrees or cutting-edge algorithms, but from the unfiltered perspective of a child who's simply eager to learn and quick to love.

So, let's step into the classroom and see what Eric has to teach us. Leadership class is in session (crayons, questions, heart and all.) Let's begin.

CHAPTER 1
The Curious Questioner
Asking Better Questions

"The important thing is not to stop questioning. Curiosity has its own reason for existing." — Albert Einstein

Eric's kindergarten classroom buzzed with activity during show-and-tell. As class leader for the day, five-year-old Eric furrowed his brow at a friend's display of a clay volcano. Instead of simply nodding along, Eric raised his hand and gently asked, "How did you make the lava?" In a few simple words, he transformed the atmosphere into one where other children leaned in, curious for the answer. The teacher smiled as the presenter eagerly explained his process. Eric's small question unlocked a deeper exploration, turning an ordinary show-and-tell into a science adventure. That afternoon, Eric learned that a leader's curiosity can inspire everyone around him to learn more.

Curiosity lies at the heart of effective leadership. In Eric's world, asking sincere questions encouraged his classmates to think creatively and share their knowledge. In the adult world, the power of asking better questions can transform teams and organizations. Great leaders often distinguish themselves not by having all the answers, but by having the courage and humility to ask the right questions. In an era dominated by artificial intelligence and rapid innovation, leaders who cultivate a childlike curiosity gain a critical edge. They create environments where exploration is valued over immediate certainty, enabling their organizations to adapt and thrive in the face of uncertainty.

Research supports the idea that curiosity drives high performance. A Harvard Business Review study found that cultivating curiosity at all levels of an organization helps leaders and employees adapt to uncertain market conditions and external pressures. When curiosity is triggered, people tend to think more deeply and rationally about decisions and come up with more creative solutions. In addition, curiosity allows leaders to gain more respect from their followers and inspires employees to develop more trusting and more collaborative relationships with colleagues. By asking thoughtful questions and encouraging others to do the same, a leader signals that learning and exploration are welcome. This not only yields smarter decisions but also fosters a culture where team members feel empowered to speak up with ideas and concerns.

In today's fast-moving business climate,

curiosity is more prized than ever. According to a recent industry survey, **83% of C-Suite executives and more than half of employees believe that curiosity sparks positive organizational change**. Despite this, many workplaces unintentionally stifle curiosity, largely because employees fear that asking questions might be seen as a lack of expertise or a challenge to authority. A five-year-old like Eric doesn't carry those fears; he asks "why?" unabashedly. Effective leaders channel that fearless inquisitiveness, asking questions that others might shy away from. By doing so, they uncover blind spots and drive innovation. After all, in an AI-driven world where information is abundant, the advantage comes from asking *better* questions, not just gathering more answers.

Leaders throughout history have recognized the value of questions. The ancient Greek philosopher Socrates taught by asking probing questions, a technique that remains effective and is still used in law schools today to train sharp-thinking attorneys. In modern business, some of the most innovative companies encourage a questioning culture. Take Toyota, for instance: its famous "Five Whys" technique insists that employees ask "why" at least five times to uncover the root cause of a problem. This practice, rooted in curiosity, helped Toyota continually improve quality and efficiency by uncovering hidden causes of issues rather than treating superficial symptoms. It's a simple example of curiosity institutionalized.

The CEO Who Asked Questions, Not Just Gave Answers

When Satya Nadella became CEO of Microsoft in 2014, he encountered a company that had grown complacent after decades of dominance. Instead of pretending to know it all, Nadella started asking questions. He famously urged Microsoft to shift from a "know-it-all" culture to a "learn-it-all" culture focused on continuous learning and listening. Consider asking engineers and managers open-ended questions, such as: *What do you think our customers really need? Why do we do it this way?*

This Socratic, curious approach was infectious. Managers began seeking input from front-line employees and customers, uncovering insights that had been overlooked. Under Nadella's leadership, Microsoft transformed by embracing curiosity and a growth mindset. Few can dispute the impact, because within a few years, Microsoft's "learn-it-all" culture contributed to the company's resurgence in innovation and market value. Nadella killed failing projects that no longer made sense, embraced promising opportunities like cloud computing, and even invested in futuristic bets like AI partnerships. By asking questions rather than dictating answers, he ignited creativity across the organization and pivoted Microsoft toward new growth areas. His tenure illustrates how a leader's genuine curiosity can rejuvenate even a giant organization and empower it to adapt and excel.

In an AI-driven world, facts and data are increasingly accessible at lightning speed. What sets great leaders apart is the ability to frame the *right* questions, the kind that a basic search engine can't easily answer.

Consider how a lawyer leading a case might ask, "What are we missing in our understanding of the client's problem?" or a tech manager might wonder, "Is there another way to achieve this that we haven't tried?" These thoughtful questions open new avenues precisely because they challenge assumptions and prompt deeper inquiry. AI can provide information, but only humans can supply the curiosity and context to use that information wisely. Like Eric marveling at a clay volcano, effective leaders remain perpetually curious about a deeper explanation. They probe beyond the obvious, encourage their teams to explore alternatives, and treat every challenge as an opportunity to learn something new.

Ask Questions Others Won't

Great leaders, like great five-year-olds, never lose their curiosity. They ask questions that others won't, especially when an answer may result in short-term discomfort, but ultimately unlock creativity and growth. As a leader, remember that your willingness to say "I don't know—let's find out" can galvanize your team. Embrace the power of the curious question, and you'll foster a culture of learning that keeps your organization adaptive and innovative on every front.

CHAPTER 2
The Listening Leader
Empathetic Listening

"Most people do not listen with the intent to understand; they listen with the intent to reply." — Stephen R. Covey

At circle time, Eric noticed his classmate Maria sitting quietly, her shoulders slumped. As the class leader, he invited her to share what was wrong. Maria hesitated, eyes downcast, then mumbled that she'd lost her favorite pencil. Some kids giggled, but Eric leaned closer and listened, really listened. He didn't interrupt or roll his eyes; he just gave her a small nod and a kind smile. The teacher watched as Maria's voice grew steadier. By the end of her story, Eric offered to help her look for the pencil during recess. Maria smiled for the first time that day. In those few minutes, five-year-old Eric discovered a profound truth: when a leader truly listens, people feel valued, and problems start to find solutions.

Empathetic listening is a cornerstone of impactful leadership. In Eric's simple act of listening without judgment, we see the seed of what adult leaders strive to achieve: making others feel heard and understood. In a professional setting, empathetic listening extends beyond merely hearing words. It involves tuning in to the emotions, concerns, and unspoken questions underlying those words. Leaders who listen empathetically build trust within their teams. People open up about challenges and ideas, knowing they won't be dismissed or ridiculed. This trust is especially critical in high-pressure fields, such as law and consulting, where team members often grapple with complex problems and tight deadlines. A leader who listens first, like Eric did for Maria, can defuse tensions, catch issues early, and show genuine care for their colleagues.

Stephen Covey, a renowned leadership author, observed that too often we listen not to understand, but to craft our reply. Empathetic leaders flip that script, focusing on understanding first. The benefits of this approach are backed by research. For instance, a survey by Catalyst found that in organizations where leaders demonstrate high empathy, nearly two-thirds of employees are innovative at work, compared to only 13% in less empathetic cultures. Empathy from leaders also drives engagement, with more than three-quarters of people whose bosses demonstrate empathy reporting feeling engaged in their jobs, compared to only one-third under less empathetic managers. The data is clear: when people feel heard and valued, they contribute more creativity and energy.

Even in the high-stakes environment of legal practice, empathy pays dividends. An attorney who truly listens to a client's anxieties and goals will not only strengthen that client's trust but also often uncover key details that shape a more effective strategy to solve their real problem (which is not always bound by the courts). By hearing what a client *really* cares about (maybe it's protecting their reputation more than the financial outcome, for instance), a lawyer can tailor their approach accordingly. The same holds for leaders in any field; empathetic listening leads to insights that a purely analytical mindset might miss.

Most importantly, empathetic listening creates psychological safety. When team members feel heard AND understood, they're more likely to speak up about problems or contribute novel ideas. This open communication loop can save organizations from disaster (imagine an employee voicing a concern that averts a project flaw) and drive innovation. Empathy also encourages reciprocal behavior, as employees tend to mirror leaders who demonstrate genuine concern. A culture of empathetic listening thus propagates itself, leading to stronger collaboration and morale at all levels.

Nelson Mandela's Legacy of Listening

One of the most powerful examples of empathetic listening in leadership comes from Nelson Mandela. Mandela often credited his skill as a leader to a lesson from his childhood, observing his father in village council meetings. His father, a tribal chief, would gather the community elders in a circle and be the last to speak. He patiently listened as everyone else shared their opinions and feelings. Only after all voices were heard would he offer his perspective, gently guiding the group toward consensus. Mandela carried this practice into his own leadership. During his presidency, he would silently absorb each minister's input, making each person feel heard, before summarizing the points and shaping the decision. By *speaking last*, Mandela cultivated immense trust. People knew he genuinely cared about their viewpoints, even if he ultimately made a different decision. This approach allowed him to unite diverse, often conflicting perspectives in post-apartheid South Africa; it was no small feat.

As leadership expert Simon Sinek explains when retelling this story, by listening first and asking questions to understand where others were coming from, Mandela made everyone feel valued and then "subtly steered" the decision in the direction he thought best. His example shows that empathetic listening isn't a "soft" skill at all; it's a leadership superpower that can rally people around a common purpose.

In a contemporary business context, the same principle applies. Consider a consulting firm's Managing Partner mediating a tense meeting between partners who disagree on a strategy. A leader who channels Mandela's "listen first" ethos would invite each attorney to share their reasoning fully, while the other listens without interruption. By acknowledging each viewpoint— *"I see why you're concerned about the client's budget"* or *"I hear that you fear this approach might risk our ability to deliver"*—the partner defuses the conflict.

Often, just feeling heard softens people's stances and opens them to compromise. Empathetic listening also helps leaders catch subtle signals: the hesitance in a junior consultant's voice that might indicate burnout, or the crack in a client's tone that reveals an unspoken worry. In an AI-augmented future, these human nuances become even more critical. While AI can analyze speech or text for keywords, it's the empathic leader who senses the emotions behind those words and responds with compassion.

Empathy in leadership can also stem from personal experience. Satya Nadella of Microsoft often cites how being the father of a child with special needs fundamentally deepened his empathy. Early in his career, Nadella admits, he was more focused on metrics and results than people's feelings. But raising his son, Zain, who had cerebral palsy, taught Nadella patience, compassion, and the importance of seeing the world through others' eyes. When he became CEO, he brought that mindset to Microsoft's culture, emphasizing empathy as a core value. He encouraged employees to *"listen more and talk less,"* and famously asked his teams to approach interactions with the mindset of *"What more can I learn?"* rather than *"Here's what I know."*

This focus on empathetic listening and understanding the perspectives of customers and colleagues helped revitalize Microsoft's morale and innovation. Products like the Xbox Adaptive Controller (designed for gamers with disabilities) were, in part, a result of this empathetic culture that valued understanding users' challenges. Nadella's story illustrates how life experiences can make a leader more attuned to others, and how that personal growth can ripple out into broader organizational change.

Listen to Understand

Before you lead, listen. Give others your full attention with the intention of understanding, not just responding. Empathetic listening isn't about staying silent; it's about making space for others to be heard. When people feel truly listened to, they give you their trust, loyalty, and best efforts. As a leader, you have the opportunity every day to be, as Covey would say, the one who seeks first to understand. Do this consistently, and you'll cultivate a team that feels seen, supported, and is willing to go the extra mile under your guidance.

CHAPTER 3
Challenging the Status Quo
Questioning Assumptions

"Your assumptions are your windows on the world. Scrub them off every once in a while, or the light won't come in." — Alan Alda

Eric's classroom was preparing for the big class play. When assigning roles, Eric immediately pointed to Jacob to be the "villain." Jacob sometimes played rough during recess, and without thinking, Eric assumed he'd fit the bad guy part. But as rehearsals began, Jacob stumbled over the angry lines and eventually burst into tears. He didn't want to be the villain at all. Eric was stunned; he had never imagined gentle Jacob could be upset by this. With his teacher's guidance, Eric apologized and asked Jacob what role he'd actually like. It turned out Jacob wanted to be the hero. They switched roles, and Jacob beamed with confidence. That day, Eric learned a humbling lesson. Assumptions can mislead a leader, and sometimes you must set them aside to let the truth shine through.

Leadership often means questioning the status quo, even when that status quo exists only in our own minds. Eric's snap judgment about his classmate is a simple example of how easily assumptions can go unchallenged. In business and law, unexamined assumptions can become costly blind spots. We fall into routines, believing *"this is how it's always done"* or *"this approach worked before, so it will work again."*

But a five-year-old's perspective reminds us to stay curious and flexible. Leaders who challenge assumptions foster innovation and avoid pitfalls. This may involve reevaluating a long-standing client strategy, questioning whether a firm's internal policy remains effective, or encouraging a team to consider an outsider's perspective. By contrast, a leader who clings to assumptions, like Eric initially did, risks making decisions based on outdated or inaccurate "truths."

Challenging assumptions is not about being contrarian for its own sake; it's about keeping our "mental windows" clean, as Alan Alda put it. Innovation thrives when we refuse to accept that the first answer or the usual method is necessarily the best.

In a study on creative leadership, researchers noted that "radical creativity" requires continuously challenging assumptions, reframing problems, and embracing new attitudes to find solutions beyond traditional boundaries. "The biggest thing holding us back is our own attitudes and the things we've learned along the way," one innovation expert said. In other words, our mental handcuffs are often self-imposed. By actively questioning our beliefs, we break free of those constraints.

This is especially vital in an AI-driven world, as technology disrupts industries, yesterday's assumptions quickly become today's antiquated beliefs. The leaders who excel are those who habitually ask, *"What if our basic premise is wrong? What if the opposite were true?"*

We see the power of challenging assumptions in the approach of visionary leaders like Elon Musk. When Musk set out to build SpaceX, he didn't accept the aerospace industry's assumption that rocket launches had to cost tens of millions of dollars each. Instead, he employed *first-principles thinking*, breaking a problem down to its fundamental truths and reasoning up from there. He asked, essentially, "What are rockets made of, and what do those raw materials cost?" By discovering that the actual materials were only a fraction of the cost of a finished rocket, Musk challenged the assumption that space travel must be prohibitively expensive. SpaceX then engineered rockets in-house from basic materials and pursued reusability, dramatically lowering costs and revolutionizing the industry. That breakthrough only happened because Musk refused to take prevailing assumptions at face value.

On the flip side, consider a more cautionary parable often told in management circles: the *"five monkeys experiment."* In this story (the origins of which are debated), scientists place five monkeys in a cage with a ladder leading to a banana, but whenever a monkey climbs the ladder, all monkeys are sprayed with cold water. Eventually, the monkeys stop anyone from climbing, even after the water stops, and new monkeys who never saw the spray are introduced. In the end, none of the monkeys climb the ladder, though none know why; it's just the way things have always been.

While not a literal scientific study, this tale

resonates because it captures how assumptions get embedded in organizational culture. Teams can end up doing things a certain way long after the original reason is gone, simply because *"that's how it's done."* A leader who challenges assumptions is the one who says, "Let's climb the ladder and see what happens," potentially discovering that the old barriers are no longer there (or never should have been in the first place).

BlackBerry's Assumptions vs. Apple's Vision

The rise and fall of BlackBerry, once a smartphone giant, offers a cautionary tale about the danger of clinging to assumptions. In the mid-2000s, BlackBerry's leaders assumed that customers would never give up the physical keyboard on their phones. Early smartphones with touchscreens, like Apple's first iPhone, were dismissed by BlackBerry executives as impractical novelties. One executive scoffed that the iPhone had "rapid battery drain and a lousy digital keyboard," reflecting a belief that no professional would want to type on a screen. Confident in their assumption that business users *needed* real keys, BlackBerry was slow to adapt to the touchscreen revolution.

Meanwhile, Steve Jobs and Apple were busy challenging the very assumption BlackBerry held sacred. Jobs asked, in essence, "Why *must* a phone have a physical keyboard? What if a screen could do it all?" By tossing out that old belief, Apple redefined the smartphone. The iPhone's success proved that consumers would happily trade buttons for a bigger screen and intuitive design. BlackBerry held faith that its unique keyboard and secure email system would be enough to retain its market share, but fundamentally, they failed to see the bigger picture and adapt to new user preferences. Within a few years, BlackBerry went from market leader to nearly irrelevant, while Apple (and later Android competitors) sped ahead.

The company's assumptions about what customers wanted, combined with its reluctance to change, led to its downfall.

By contrast, leaders at Apple and Google thrived by questioning assumptions. Google's founders challenged the assumption that a home page had to be cluttered (remember how sparse and clean Google's search page was compared to early competitors). That clarity helped them dominate the search. Netflix's leaders (as we'll see in Chapter 6) challenged the assumption that people preferred video rental stores, which led them to a streaming model that upended an industry. In each case, tossing out the conventional wisdom opened the door to creativity and success.

This dynamic plays out beyond tech gadgets. Consider a corporate law firm that always staffs cases the same way because, historically, that's how they've won. One day, a junior partner suggests using an AI tool for initial contract review. The old assumption might be, "AI can't do what a seasoned attorney does." But by challenging that, the firm could discover a new efficiency, freeing up lawyers to focus on strategy rather than paperwork. Many firms that failed to question their assumptions (such as early perceptions that remote work could never be effective for client services) found themselves scrambling when circumstances changed. On the other hand, those who proactively ask, "Why not?" adapt quickly and gain a competitive edge.

Break Your Assumptions

Progress in any field comes from leaders willing to say, "Maybe our assumptions are wrong." Don't let "we've always done it this way" become a blind spot. Instead, channel your inner five-year-old and ask why, why, why. Scrub your mental windows to let in fresh light. By challenging assumptions, you keep yourself and your organization open to new possibilities.

In a rapidly changing world, the ability to rethink and unlearn is just as important as the ability to learn. Free yourself and your team from outdated beliefs, and you'll find that innovation and improvement often lie just on the other side of a broken assumption.

CHAPTER 4
All for One
Collaborative Decision-Making

"If you want to go fast, go alone. If you want to go far, go together." — African Proverb

On a sunny morning, Eric's teacher announced it was time for the class to choose a game for the activity period. Immediately, a chorus of voices shouted their favorites: tag, drawing, building blocks, hide-and-seek. As class leader, Eric felt overwhelmed. He started by picking his own favorite game (tag), assuming everyone would just follow along. But half the class groaned, and two friends started arguing that hide-and-seek was better.

Remembering what it felt like when his assumption about Jacob was wrong, Eric paused. He gathered his classmates in a circle (just like he'd seen his teacher do) and asked each to share one game they'd love to play. After hearing everyone out, they voted and agreed on a game that combined tag *and* hide-and-seek in a new way. For the rest of that period, laughter and excitement filled the playground. Eric beamed with pride, realizing that by involving everyone in the decision, they created something more fun than any one person's idea.

Collaborative decision-making involves harnessing the collective wisdom of the group, rather than relying solely on a single leader's preference. In Eric's simple scenario, the pivot from "my way" to "our way" transformed a potential conflict into a creative solution.

In the adult world, the stakes are higher. Project directions, client strategies, and even entire organizational changes, but the principle remains. When people have a voice in decisions that affect them, the outcomes are often better and the buy-in far greater. No one enjoys edicts handed down from on high, especially if they feel their own insights were ignored. Leaders in professional settings find that when they foster a culture of collaboration, teams become more engaged and committed to the chosen path. It doesn't mean every decision is made by committee or consensus, but it does mean that people are heard, and their perspectives are considered before the leader charts the course.

The benefits of involving your team in decision-making are well-documented. Research indicates that organizations with inclusive, collaborative leadership see significantly higher employee engagement and performance. One study found that when employees are involved in the decision-making process, they feel more valued and invested in the outcome, resulting in substantially better results for the organization.

Highly engaged employees produce better outcomes, are likelier to stay at their organization, and experience less burnout. Another survey revealed a striking statistic: 86% of employees and executives attributed workplace failures to a lack of collaboration or ineffective communication. Think about that.

Almost nine out of ten times, when things fall apart, it's not due to lack of technical skills or knowledge, but because people didn't work together effectively. That underscores a simple truth: *a team that decides together thrives together.* By contrast, top-down decisions made in a vacuum can breed resentment or half-hearted compliance. Collaborative decision-making, even if it takes a bit more time upfront, pays off with stronger execution and a united team pulling in the same direction.

History provides dramatic examples of collaboration saving the day. During the Apollo 13 space mission in 1970, an oxygen tank exploded en route to the Moon, crippling the spacecraft. The three astronauts' lives were in grave danger as carbon dioxide levels rose, and power dwindled. At NASA's Mission Control, Flight Director Gene Kranz didn't single-handedly come up with a solution. Instead, he galvanized a *team* of engineers and experts in a feverish collaboration. Famously, the team working on the CO_2 problem dumped a pile of random spacecraft parts onto a table (hoses, duct tape, canisters, etc.) and collaboratively figured out how to jury-rig a square CO_2 filter into a round hole using only those materials.

Through open brainstorming and pooled expertise, they achieved the impossible under pressure, and Apollo 13's crew returned safely to Earth. In the debrief, Kranz noted that it was the trust and cooperation among his flight controllers that turned potential tragedy into what he called *"our finest hour."* The Apollo 13 saga, albeit in extreme circumstances, highlights how collaborative decision-making harnesses collective genius. No single expert had the answer; it took contributions from many minds, building on each other's ideas, to bring the astronauts home. This is the power of collaboration; it can literally solve problems that no individual can solve alone.

Ford's Turnaround through Teamwork

When Alan Mulally took over as CEO of Ford in 2006, the automaker was in dire straits. Ford's culture had been notoriously siloed and cutthroat; executives prioritized their own advancement and the success of their own departments over the bottom line. The company was divided into warring fiefdoms, and little collaboration occurred across divisions. Mulally recognized that no turnaround would succeed unless he could get leaders to collaborate rather than compete internally. He instituted a new practice: a weekly executive meeting where all VPs had to openly share the status of their projects, using green, yellow, or red indicators to indicate performance.

Initially, everyone reported "green" across the board, despite the company's financial struggles. Why? Because they were afraid to admit problems in front of their peers. Mulally made it safe to be honest.

In one meeting, when an executive finally confessed to a major issue (a "red flag" on a vehicle launch), Mulally thanked them and then asked the room, *"Who can help him with that?"* This was a radical departure from the blame games of the past.

By explicitly tying each leader's performance evaluation to Ford's overall success (one team, one goal), Mulally broke down the walls between fiefdoms. Soon, leaders started solving problems together. If manufacturing had a delay, product development and marketing would step in to help, rather than pointing fingers.

Ford's employees often cite the "One Ford" ethos, where everyone works toward a shared vision, as a key reason the company survived the 2008 financial crisis without a government bailout. Applying the same collaborative methods he used at Boeing years before, Mulally transformed Ford's cutthroat, siloed culture into a model of teamwork and transparency. The results were evident in Ford's return to profitability and improvements in product quality. The man who saved Ford did not do it by making heroic solo decisions, but by getting everyone to pull together. The Ford story illustrates a broader lesson: *Collaboration amplifies impact.*

In professional services firms, similarly, a partner might insist on cross-departmental meetings for major client proposals, ensuring that, for instance, both the litigation and corporate teams contribute to a client's solution. This collaborative approach often uncovers risks and overlapping opportunities that a single team might miss, and it fosters a sense of shared ownership in the client's success. It might slow the process down slightly (meetings and consensus-building do take time), but it nearly always leads to a more robust outcome and a united team ready to execute it. And as the African proverb reminds us, *if you want to go far, go together.*

Collaboration is essentially an act of humility, acknowledging that none of us is as smart as all of us. Leaders who practice it create cultures of mutual respect and shared purpose. Many companies have learned to involve employees from different levels in decision-making processes for significant changes. This will become even more of a superpower in the era of AI development and adoption.

Take, for example, a global consulting firm. A senior manager might crowdsource ideas from junior consultants on improving a service offering. The juniors, being closer to the day-to-day work, often highlight issues or client feedback that leadership may have missed. When those ideas are folded into the final decision, implementation goes smoother because the people doing the work had a hand in shaping it.

Nearly 75% of employers rate teamwork and collaboration as "very important," yet a significant portion of employees feel their organizations don't collaborate enough. The role of the leader is to bridge that gap, intentionally design processes (such as Mulally's meetings or cross-functional project teams) that encourage collaboration to happen, until it becomes second nature.

A Collaborative Journey

Don't be the leader who goes it alone. Be the one who gathers the team, values their input, and decides *with* them, not just *for* them. Collaborative decision-making isn't a sign of weakness or indecision; it's a strategy for getting it right and getting everyone on board. By involving others and genuinely listening to their perspectives, you make better decisions and foster a sense of unity and ownership. The journey might be slower at first, especially when you embrace the power of a pause, but the destination will be that much more rewarding, and you won't be arriving there alone.

CHAPTER 5
Calm in the Storm
Conflict Resolution

"Conflict is inevitable, but combat is optional." — Max Lucado

The art corner in Eric's classroom was normally a place of pride, where crayon drawings and finger paintings hung for all to admire. One afternoon, Eric discovered two classmates, Asha and Leo, shouting near a ripped painting. Asha accused Leo of tearing her artwork, and Leo yelled that it was an accident. Tears were welling up. As the class leader, Eric felt panic at first. This was a real clash, and he was just five! But he remembered how listening helped Maria and how questions helped with the game choice.

So Eric gently separated his friends and spoke softly: *"Asha, what happened? Leo, you too."* He listened as each vented, Asha through sobs and Leo through an angry frown. It turned out Leo had bumped the drying rack by mistake. Asha thought it was on purpose. Eric suggested they work together to fix the painting with tape and even add some new drawings to cover the tear. By cleanup time, Asha and Leo were chatting again, proudly showing off their "mixed-up masterpiece." Eric learned that day that stepping into a conflict calmly could turn a crisis into a creative solution.

Every leader, no matter how cheerful or well-intentioned, will face conflict. It's as inevitable as a playground argument or a heated disagreement in a boardroom. The difference between a thriving team and a toxic one is not the absence of conflict, but how conflict is managed. Eric's instinctual approach in the art corner (to listen to both sides, seek understanding, and find a constructive way forward) is a template that scales remarkably well to adult scenarios.

In the professional world, unresolved conflicts can fester and blow up, derailing projects and damaging relationships. Conversely, conflicts handled with empathy and fairness can actually strengthen trust and spark improvement (much like how Asha and Leo ended up jointly improving the artwork that caused their fight).

Unfortunately, many workplaces shy away from conflict or handle it poorly. The costs of avoidance or mismanagement are huge. Studies show that U.S. employees spend an average of 2.8 hours per week dealing with conflict, which amounts to approximately $359 billion in paid hours per year lost to workplace discord. Put another way, that's like every employee in the country spending one day a month essentially unproductive due to conflict. Notably, a majority of employees (54%) believe that managers could resolve disagreements more effectively by addressing tensions *immediately when they arise*, rather than waiting.

This highlights the importance of timely intervention; small fires are easier to extinguish than big ones. Small wonder, then, that 70% of employees consider conflict management a critically important leadership skill. Left unchecked, minor disagreements can escalate into team-dividing disputes or costly turnover (as people leave to escape a toxic environment). As Max Lucado's quote reminds us, conflict will happen, but leaders get to choose whether it turns into combative, harmful battles or opportunities for dialogue and resolution. Effective conflict resolution doesn't mean everyone ends up agreeing or even happy; rather, it means the issue is addressed in a respectful, productive way so the team can move forward together.

Eric's approach maps well to proven conflict

resolution techniques. He separated the people from the problem (cooling Asha and Leo down individually first), listened to understand (letting each person tell their story without interruption), and then guided them toward a joint solution (fixing the painting together). In management terms, this is akin to a mediation process. The leader acts as a neutral facilitator, ensuring each party feels heard and then refocusing them on a common goal (solving the problem, not attacking each other). By doing so, the leader transforms the conflict from a personal clash into a shared challenge that needs to be overcome.

Sometimes conflict isn't just between colleagues; it can erupt between an organization and the public. In 2018, Starbucks faced a firestorm when two Black men were arrested at a Philadelphia Starbucks store while simply waiting for a friend. The incident, which was seen as an instance of racial bias, sparked national outrage, a form of social conflict that could have severely damaged the company's reputation and trust with customers. Starbucks CEO Kevin Johnson responded with a conflict resolution mindset scaled to an entire enterprise. He swiftly issued a sincere public apology, took personal responsibility, and then made a bold decision: Starbucks would close all 8,000+ U.S. company-owned stores for an afternoon to conduct racial bias training for 175,000 employees.

This was an unprecedented move, essentially saying, "We hear you, and we're going to address the root of this conflict." By tackling the issue head-on, acknowledging the hurt, and investing in education, Starbucks successfully turned a public relations crisis into an opportunity to reinforce its values. While not everyone was satisfied, many observers noted that Starbucks's proactive and empathetic approach likely prevented deeper, long-term damage to the brand. The lesson for leaders is that conflict resolution skills aren't just for internal spats;

they are crucial when addressing conflicts with customers, communities, or stakeholders at large. Johnson's approach mirrored the principles we've discussed. He listened to the public outcry, engaged with experts and employees on solutions, and took transparent action to remedy the situation.

Turning Conflict into Collaboration

Consider a scenario from a global consulting firm. Two senior managers, Kim and Alejandro, were leading different teams bidding on a massive client project. Instead of collaborating, they began undermining each other, each convinced their approach was superior. Tensions rose; team members took sides. The conflict was on the verge of losing the firm a lucrative client because the internal rivalry was delaying the proposal. The firm's director stepped in as a leader (aka, mediator).

In a joint meeting, she established ground rules: each manager would fully explain their perspective, while the other listened without interruption. Kim shared her concerns about Alejandro's timeline being unrealistic; Alejandro revealed he felt Kim's plan was too cautious and might bore the client. Through this facilitated discussion, they discovered a middle ground, combining Kim's risk management steps with Alejandro's ambitious vision. The final proposal, born from the resolution of their conflict, was stronger than either of the originals. They won the client contract and, perhaps more importantly, Kim and Alejandro emerged with newfound respect for each other's skills. The director's willingness to confront the conflict directly, rather than letting it fester or declaring a top-down verdict, exemplified conflict resolution at its best. She treated the dispute not as a personal feud to be stamped out, but as a problem to be solved collectively.

In doing so, she turned a potential losing situation into a win-win. Both managers felt heard and valued, and their teams saw a positive example of resolving differences through dialogue. Moreover, the organization preserved the client opportunity and actually delivered a better outcome because the conflict forced them to integrate two approaches. The moral of the story: a leader skilled in conflict resolution can transform friction into fuel for better performance.

In an era of virtual teams and cross-cultural workforces, conflict may not always announce itself with a shouting match. It might be a passive-aggressive email thread or a silent tension on a conference call. Leaders must remain vigilant and proactive. Embracing conflict resolution means not seeing disagreements as threats to your authority, but as natural occurrences that, when handled well, can lead to better understanding or innovation.

For example, two department heads might clash over budget allocations. A leader with a mediator's mindset will bring them together, facilitate a fact-based yet respectful discussion, and perhaps discover a creative way to satisfy both (e.g., like a resource-sharing agreement) rather than declaring one the winner and the other the loser. By modeling calm, curiosity, and fairness when conflicts arise, you set a tone that problems are meant to be solved, not hidden. People learn that on this team, issues don't fester; we face them together.

Conflict is an Opportunity That Needs to be Understood

Conflict is a fact of life, but as a leader, you have the choice to make it either destructive or transformative. Don't avoid it, address it. Stay calm, listen to all sides, and guide the parties toward common ground. Remember that conflict isn't a contest to be won; it's a problem to be understood and solved. When you intervene with empathy and fairness, conflicts become lessons instead of landmines. By handling disputes openly and effectively, you build a culture where people trust that even when they disagree, they won't be vilified or ignored. They'll be heard, and together you'll find a way forward. Be the leader who puts out fires, not one who ignites them.

CHAPTER 6
Riding the Winds of Change

Navigating Change

"When the wind of change blows, some build walls, while others build windmills."
— Chinese proverb

The classroom felt different on Monday morning. Over the weekend, the beloved class pet hamster, Fuzzy, was adopted by a permanent family. When the teacher gently broke the news, a few children looked as though they were on the verge of tears. Fuzzy had been a comforting constant. Even Eric felt his throat tighten; he'd grown used to greeting the little furball each day. Seeing his classmates' distress, Eric took a deep breath and did something unexpected for a five-year-old. He asked the teacher if they could make a goodbye card for Fuzzy and maybe brainstorm a new class project to fill the empty spot. The teacher loved the idea.

By day's end, the class had not only created a colorful card, but they had also decided to start a small class garden in the window where Fuzzy's cage once sat. Watering seeds each day gave them a new shared purpose. Eric learned that while change can be sad or scary, a leader can help others navigate it by honoring what was lost and finding hope in what's next.

Change is the only constant, as the saying goes, but that doesn't make it easy. Whether it's a pet leaving a classroom or a major reorganization in a firm, change inevitably stirs emotions: fear, uncertainty, sometimes excitement.

Leaders are the ones people look to in those moments of upheaval.

Eric's small act, channeling the class's energy into a constructive response, mirrors what effective leaders do in the face of change. They acknowledge the feelings of the group (the sadness over Fuzzy's departure) and help people find a path forward (the new class garden). Navigating change is about providing stability in the midst of uncertainty. It might involve crafting a vision of the future that people can rally around, or simply offering empathy and clarity when routines are upended. Crucially, it's about being proactive and building windmills, not walls, when the winds of change blow. The leader who resists or ignores change is trying to "build a wall" to keep things as they were; they risk being swept away when the winds inevitably strengthen.

The corporate landscape is littered with examples of poor change management. It's commonly estimated (and debated) that 70%

of change initiatives fail, leaving organizations scrambling to recover lost time, money, and employee trust. Why such a high failure rate? Research suggests a gap between leaders' intentions and employees' experiences during change. One study found that while 74% of leaders believe they actively include employees in shaping change strategies, only 42% of employees feel they actually have a say in creating change. This disconnect leads to cynicism and resistance.

To navigate change successfully, leaders must close that gap by engaging people early and often. When employees are active participants in change, their buy-in soars. Indeed, intent to stay with an organization increases by 46% when employees are actively engaged in major change initiatives. Open communication and inclusive planning can mean the difference between a change that flops and one that flourishes. These numbers tell a clear story: change imposed on people breeds pushback, but change built *with* people can spark enthusiasm and commitment.

Change guru John Kotter emphasizes that successful transformations require leaders to communicate a clear vision, empower people to act, and celebrate short-term wins to build momentum. In practice, this means painting a compelling picture of the future (the windmill you're building), removing obstacles that hold people back, and acknowledging progress to maintain high morale.

A recent and relatable example of navigating change was the sudden shift to remote work during the COVID-19 pandemic in 2020. Practically overnight, companies around the world had to uproot traditional office-based routines and go fully virtual. Some leaders initially resisted, hoping to wait it out or worrying that productivity would collapse outside the office walls. Others embraced the change, communicating clearly with their teams, providing resources for home offices, and establishing new norms to keep everyone connected. The difference in outcomes was striking.

Organizations whose leaders facilitated the transition with empathy, acknowledging employees' childcare struggles or mental stress, and giving flexibility, often saw productivity maintained or even improved, as well as a surge in appreciation and loyalty from employees. By contrast, companies that fought the change or conveyed mistrust (for example, instituting draconian monitoring of remote workers) suffered drops in morale and, in some cases, higher turnover once the job market stabilized. This real-world "wind of change" forced everyone's hand; the leaders who built windmills were those who quickly reimagined how work could get done, rather than yearning for the return of yesterday's normal. Many found that, with the right support, their teams could indeed thrive in a new configuration, and they've kept elements of remote or hybrid work since, using it as a strategic advantage in talent retention and operational resilience.

Netflix's Reinvention (and Kodak's Missed Turn)

In the early 2000s, Netflix was a DVD-by-mail rental service. The leadership at Netflix noticed the winds of technological change beginning to gust, broadband internet was becoming widespread, and streaming technology was improving. While their then-rival Blockbuster doubled down on physical video stores (essentially building a wall against digital change), Netflix decided to build a windmill. CEO Reed Hastings made the bold move to pivot Netflix's business model to streaming video over the internet. This was a massive change, not just for customers but for Netflix's employees and infrastructure. How did he navigate it internally? By clearly articulating a vision that *"streaming is the future of entertainment,"* and involving teams across the company to experiment and learn in the new domain.

The company gradually introduced streaming alongside its DVD service, gathered feedback, and improved the platform. Netflix's culture of transparency meant that employees understood *why* the change was necessary (even if it threatened the familiar DVD business) and were empowered to contribute ideas on how to execute it. The pivot wasn't without hiccups; there were technical challenges and customer adjustments, but because Netflix's leadership navigated the change proactively and communicatively, the company not only survived the shift but became a pioneer in a whole new industry. The result is history: Netflix transformed into a global streaming giant, while Blockbuster was unable or unwilling to adapt and went bankrupt.

Contrast that with Kodak, the iconic film company. Kodak actually invented the first digital camera in the 1970s, but its leaders were so afraid of changing their core film business that they shelved the technology for years. They assumed people would never abandon film. By the time Kodak acknowledged the digital wave, it was too late; the company filed for bankruptcy in 2012 after losing relevance. Kodak's downfall is often cited as a classic case of corporate myopia. The company was *aware* of the technological change but couldn't bring itself to pivot, fearing it would cannibalize their highly profitable film sales. They built walls, hoping to defend their legacy products, while competitors and new startups built windmills by embracing digital imaging.

The lesson? Embracing change early and decisively (like Netflix did) can be a springboard to new success, whereas clinging to the past (like Kodak did) can sink even the mightiest incumbent. And for the people within those companies, it's far better to work for a leader who navigates change with courage and inclusion than one who denies or fights it until crisis hits.

In professional services, navigating change may involve a law firm adopting new AI-driven research tools or a consulting partnership restructuring to enter a new market. These shifts can be unsettling. People worry about their roles, their capabilities, and the firm's identity. Leaders who handle it well do what Eric did, they acknowledge what's being lost (perhaps an old way of working or the comfort of routine) and then actively involve their team in shaping the path forward (for example, launching training programs for the new AI tool, holding open forums to discuss the reorg, inviting feedback on transition plans).

A managing partner might say, *"This change is big, and I know it's not easy. Let's talk about your concerns, and let's also talk about what this could open up for us."* By validating emotions and inviting participation, the leader helps everyone not only cope with change but also find opportunities in it.

Leaders who navigate change effectively also take care to provide short-term wins to encourage people. Maybe it's a pilot project that demonstrates the benefit of a new process, or an interim milestone that everyone can celebrate. These wins are like the first rotations of a windmill; they prove that the structure works and generate initial energy to keep everyone motivated.

For instance, if a firm is transitioning to a new software system, a leader might highlight a small victory: *"This week we processed 20% more cases using the new system than we did with the old one. Great job, team!"* That acknowledgement builds confidence that the change is positive and working.

Change is Inevitable, Growth is Optional

As a leader, you set the tone. Will you resist the winds of change, or will you harness them?

Choose to be the leader who guides others through uncertainty by painting a clear vision and involving them in the journey. When people see you embracing change, acknowledging the challenges, but focusing on the possibilities, they're more likely to come along rather than dig in their heels. Build windmills, not walls. In doing so, you'll ensure that your team not only survives change but thrives because of it.

Lifting Others
Mentoring and Developing Talent

"The delicate balance of mentoring someone is not creating them in your own image, but giving them the opportunity to create themselves." — Steven Spielberg

It was reading time, and Eric noticed that his friend Sophie was struggling over some words in a picture book. Sophie's cheeks were red with embarrassment as other kids breezed through their books. As class leader, Eric quietly scooted closer to Sophie. Remembering how older kids had helped him tie his shoes last year, he gently whispered, *"I can help if you want."* Sophie nodded timidly. Eric didn't read the words for her; instead, he pointed at the tricky word and broke it into smaller sounds, just like their teacher had shown them. Sophie pronounced it slowly, then grinned as she got it right. Eric gave her a thumbs-up and stayed by her side through the rest of the story. By the final page, Sophie's confidence was visibly higher, and she asked Eric if they could read together again tomorrow. In that moment, Eric discovered the joy of helping someone else grow, a small act of mentoring that made both of them feel proud and capable.

The journey from a good professional to a great leader involves a pivotal shift from focusing on your own success to investing in the success of others. Mentoring is the epitome of that shift. In Eric's simple act of peer support, we see the essence of mentorship, guiding someone gently, without taking over, so they can develop their own abilities. For adult leaders, mentoring can mean formally coaching a junior colleague or simply taking a nurturing interest in the growth of those around you. It's about sharing knowledge, yes, but also about inspiring confidence.

A mentor doesn't seek to clone themselves (as Spielberg's quote warns); instead, they help the mentee discover and hone *their own* strengths. In the context of a law firm, a mentoring partner might help a young associate not by dictating how to write a brief but by providing feedback, encouragement, and opportunities for the associate to stretch their skills. In tech or consulting, a team lead might pair a new hire with challenging tasks, offering guidance along the way, so the newcomer learns by doing and gains confidence through achievement.

The impact of mentorship is profound. Studies in organizational psychology have found that employees with strong mentors report higher job satisfaction, greater organizational commitment, and even enjoy faster career progression (more promotions and higher compensation) than those without mentors. It makes sense: a mentor can open doors, offer advice to avoid pitfalls, and serve as a sounding board during tough decisions. But beyond the tangible career benefits, there's a deep human element. When someone more experienced believes in you and devotes time to help you grow, it reinforces your sense of belonging and purpose in the organization. This is why companies with mentorship programs often see better retention rates; people are more likely to stay where they feel supported and see a path for development. Conversely, in environments without mentorship, young professionals can feel adrift or undervalued, which may lead them to seek growth opportunities elsewhere.

Interestingly, mentors often report that they gain as much as they give: increased pride and job satisfaction, improved leadership skills from teaching others, and a sense of legacy in seeing their protégés succeed. By mentoring, leaders reinforce their own knowledge and hone their interpersonal skills. It creates a virtuous cycle; mentorship builds better leaders on both sides of the relationship. The mentor-mentee bond can also break down silos in an organization. A senior leader mentoring someone in a different department, for example, creates cross-pollination of knowledge and a shared understanding that can benefit the broader company.

The "Trillion Dollar Coach"

One of the most celebrated mentors in the business world was Bill Campbell, a man so influential as a coach and mentor to Silicon Valley executives that he earned the nickname "Trillion Dollar Coach." Campbell was a former football coach turned executive who mentored a roster of tech luminaries, including Steve Jobs at Apple, Larry Page and Sergey Brin at Google, Eric Schmidt of Google/Alphabet, Jeff Bezos at Amazon, and Sheryl Sandberg at

Facebook, among others. What made Campbell's mentorship extraordinary was not that he imposed his own style on these leaders, but that he helped them become the best versions of themselves. He was known for his world-class listening skills, his no-nonsense feedback delivered with love, and his knack for asking probing questions that prompted self-reflection.

For example, when Eric Schmidt struggled with managing Google's rapid growth, Campbell guided him with questions and personal anecdotes rather than strict directives, helping Schmidt find his own management rhythm. Campbell would sit in on Google's executive staff meetings, not to command, but to observe dynamics and offer quietly whispered counsel to the leaders afterwards. He built relationships on trust and genuine care, attending his mentees' family events, remembering personal details, and always being available for a tough conversation. The outcomes speak for themselves: the collective market value of companies coached by Bill Campbell reached well into the trillions, and many of those leaders openly credit Campbell's mentorship as a key ingredient in their success.

Perhaps just as important, those he mentored often became mentors to others, spreading Campbell's human-centered leadership ethos throughout the tech industry. Bill Campbell's legacy underlines a powerful truth: by lifting others, a leader can indirectly achieve far more than they ever could alone. His influence endures as his mentees mentor the next generation, creating a multiplier effect of positive leadership.

In more everyday terms, think of a senior attorney who takes a promising young lawyer under her wing. She doesn't just assign tasks; she provides context on *why* a strategy worked or didn't, shares stories of her own early mistakes, and pushes the young lawyer into challenging situations (with a safety net) to build their confidence. Over time, that associate might flourish into a star performer or even a future partner, and they'll often attribute their growth to that mentor's guidance. This cascading development is how organizations build a legacy of leadership. Each generation of leaders cultivates the next through mentorship.

Mentoring doesn't always flow top-down, either. The practice of *reverse mentoring*, popularized by General Electric CEO Jack Welch in 1999, flips the traditional model by having junior employees mentor senior executives in areas where the juniors have more expertise. In Welch's case, he paired hundreds of his top managers with young, tech-savvy employees to teach the executives about new internet technologies. This bold initiative acknowledged that even leaders have much to learn, and that young people can be a source of insight in rapidly changing fields. The result was a two-way street where the executives accelerated their learning curve on emerging digital trends, and the junior mentors gained exposure to high-level thinking and felt valued for their knowledge.

Many organizations have since adopted reverse mentoring to bridge generational gaps in skills and perspectives. The underlying message aligns perfectly with our theme: no matter how senior you are, maintaining a learning mindset (as a mentor or a mentee) is key to growth. By fostering an environment where everyone can both teach and learn, leaders demonstrate humility and a commitment to continual development for themselves and their teams.

In a world dominated by AI, mentoring assumes new dimensions. Seasoned professionals might find themselves reverse-mentored by younger colleagues on digital trends or tools, while still imparting timeless wisdom in return. The key is the two-way learning mindset: mentors learn too. By teaching others, leaders reinforce their own knowledge and stay sharp. It fosters a culture where asking for help or guidance is not viewed as a weakness by seniors or juniors, but rather as a normal part of work life. That's incredibly important when technology is evolving quickly; everyone will need to learn from everyone.

Steven Spielberg's quote about the balance of mentoring resonates here: the goal is not to mold carbon copies, but to help each person you mentor become their own success story. Do that, and your influence as a leader will extend far beyond your individual reach, echoing in the accomplishments of others for years to come. It's the difference between being a solo performer and being a teacher whose students go on to achieve great things, thereby multiplying your legacy.

The Ripple Effect

Leadership isn't just about what *you* achieve; it's measured by what you help others achieve. Make it part of your mission to lift others up, teach, coach, guide, and inspire. Be generous with your knowledge and patient with mistakes (remember, someone likely did the same for you). In doing so, you create a ripple effect of growth. Your mentees will carry forward your lessons, perhaps even surpassing you, an outcome any true leader welcomes. Mentoring also keeps you learning and growing. As you climb, reach back. There is no more enduring legacy for a leader than the people they've empowered to climb higher.

Conclusion

Leadership is a journey that doesn't end at a destination, but continuously loops back on itself as we learn, grow, stumble, and rise. In these pages, we followed Eric through the simple world of a kindergarten classroom, only to find that his experiences echo in the complex arenas of adult leadership.

From curiosity to mentorship, each chapter illuminated a facet of leadership that is both timeless and timely. Timeless, because human nature and the power of connection haven't changed. Timely, because in an age of AI and the breakneck pace of change, these human-centric skills have taken on renewed importance as our differentiators.

You might be reflecting on your own career or current leadership role, drawing parallels with Eric's stories and the examples we discussed. Perhaps you've recognized moments where you, too, asked a question that changed the trajectory of a project, or listened to a colleague in distress and strengthened a relationship. Maybe you've been the one to challenge a stale assumption and ignite innovation, or to bring a team together to make a tough decision. You may have navigated turbulent changes or taken a young talent under your wing. If so, you've already been a five-year-old leader at heart. The aim of this book was not to introduce radically new theories, but to remind you of the powerful fundamentals you already carry within, and to encourage you to use them more intentionally.

The corporate world often emphasizes metrics, algorithms, and strategies (and indeed, our references and real-world cases in this book highlight evidence and outcomes). But at its core, leadership is deeply personal and human. It's about relationships, building them, nurturing them, guiding them.

A curious question can open someone's mind; a sincere listen can heal someone's heart. A bold idea can challenge an industry; a collaborative spirit can unite a fractured team. A compassionate resolution can prevent a minor issue from escalating into a major blowup; an adaptive mindset can help an organization navigate upheaval. And a caring mentor can shape not just one career, but many, as knowledge and confidence pass from person to person, generation to generation.

In calling this book *The 5-Year-Old CEO*, we honor the idea that greatness in leadership doesn't always wear a suit or speak in polished rhetoric. Sometimes, it wears sneakers and speaks from the heart. The future of leadership, especially in an AI-driven world, belongs to those who are willing to stay endlessly curious, relentlessly empathetic, and bravely imaginative. Technology will continue to evolve and astound us, but it will be the curious questioner, the compassionate listener, the open-minded challenger, the team collaborator, the conflict peacemaker, the change navigator, and the people builder who ensure those technologies are used to create value and positive impact.

As you close this book, my hope is that you carry forward not only the lessons but the spirit behind them. The next time you face a leadership challenge, big or small, think of Eric with his hand raised, asking "why?", or sitting quietly, ears open to a friend. Think of the fearlessness of a child who doesn't yet know to be cynical, who believes every problem has a solution if only we care enough to find it. That mindset, combined with your professional expertise and experience, is a formidable force.

Remember, leadership is not a title bestowed; it's an action taken. It's available to anyone in any role, at any stage of their career. You can start practicing these principles right now, exactly where you are. Ask more questions in your next meeting. Take an extra moment to hear someone out today. Challenge an assumption that's begging to be tested. Invite a colleague into a decision you'd normally make alone. Extend a hand to someone who could use guidance. These small acts, done consistently, transform not just organizations but people's lives.

In the grand tale of leadership, each of us is both student and teacher. Like Eric, we learn from those around us and, in turn, illuminate the path for others. The power of curiosity, empathy, and innovation lives within you. Nurture it, share it, and watch it cascade through your team, your company, your community.

Lead with the wide eyes of a child and the wise heart of an adult. That is the balance of

The 5-Year-Old CEO. In doing so, you'll not only navigate the challenges of an AI-driven world, but you'll also shape a better, more human future within it.

References

1. Gino, F. (2018). *The Business Case for Curiosity*. Harvard Business Review, 96(5), 48–57. Retrieved from https://hbr.org/2018/09/the-business-case-for-curiosity

2. Wells, R. (2023, December 17). *3 Reasons Curiosity Is an In-Demand Leadership Skill – and How to Build It*. Forbes. Retrieved from https://www.forbes.com/sites/rachelwells/2023/12/17/3-reasons-curiosity-is-an-in-demand-leadership-skill-how-to-build-it/

3. Mehta, S. (2024, June 3). *Satya Nadella's 3-Word Description of Microsoft's Culture Should Inspire Leaders to Be Learners*. Inc.

Retrieved from https://www.inc.com/
stephanie-mehta/satya-nadella-on-lead-
ers-becoming-learners.html

4.   Rivonia Premier Lodge. (2020, January 31).
"Be the last one to speak" – Nelson Mandela.
[Blog post]. Retrieved from https://www.
rivoniabb.co.za/blog/last-one-speak-
nelson-mandela/

5.   Broom, D. (2021, October 11). *This is the
most important skill for a leader to have right
now.* World Economic Forum. Retrieved
from https://www.weforum.org/stories/2021/
10/secret-great-leadership-empathy/

6.   Wu, R. (2022, May 6). *BlackBerry: Assumptions and failures.* Medium. Retrieved from
https://medium.com/@rachaelcarmen
wu/reflection-point-assumptions-and-
failures-b9d3a97887fd

7.   Typpö, A. (2025, March 3). *Leadership and
Creative Disruption: The Path to Innovation.*

Aalto Leaders' Insight. Retrieved from https://www.aaltoee.fi/en/aalto-leaders-insight/2025/leadership-and-creative-disruption-the-path-to-innovation

8. Harvard Business School Online. (n.d.). *Why Managers Should Involve Their Team in Decision-Making*. Retrieved from https://online.hbs.edu/blog/post/team-decision-making

9. Hoffman, B. G. (2012, March 12). *Saving an Iconic Brand: Five Ways Alan Mulally Changed Ford's Culture*. Fast Company. Retrieved from https://www.fastcompany.com/1680075/saving-an-iconic-brand-five-ways-alan-mulally-changed-ford-s-culture

10. Short, R. (2021, November 10). *The Cost of Workplace Conflict*. Workplace Peace Institute. (Updated August 6, 2024). Retrieved from https://www.workplacepeaceinstitute.com/post/the-cost-of-workplace-conflict

11. Pollack, J. (2025, April 6). *59 Change Management Statistics.* Pollack Peacebuilding Systems. Retrieved from https://pollackpeacebuilding.com/blog/change-management-statistics/

12. Goldberg, J. (2016, July 30). *It Takes a Village to Determine the Origins of an African Proverb.* NPR. Retrieved from https://www.npr.org/2016/07/30/487925796/it-takes-a-village-to-determine-the-origins-of-an-african-proverb

13. World Economic Forum. (2019, August 29). *10 of Albert Einstein's Best Quotes.* Retrieved from https://www.weforum.org/agenda/2019/08/albert-einstein-quotes-inspiring-clever-funny-famous/

14. Covey, S. R. (1989). *The 7 Habits of Highly Effective People: Powerful Lessons in Personal Change.* New York, NY: Free Press.

15. Goodreads. (n.d.). Quote by Alan Alda: "Your assumptions are your windows on the world . . .". Retrieved from https://www.goodreads.com/quotes/667214-your-assumptions-are-your-windows-on-the-world-scrub-them

16. Goodreads. (n.d.). Quote by Max Lucado: "Conflict is inevitable, but combat is optional." Retrieved from https://www.goodreads.com/quotes/500588-conflict-is-inevitable-but-combat-is-optional

17. Sim, J. (2014, November 3). *002: Chinese Proverb – When The Wind Of Change Blows*. Rational Comics. Retrieved from https://www.rationalcomics.com/002-when-the-wind-of-change-blows/

18. The Foundation for a Better Life. (n.d.). *Inspirational Quote by Steven Spielberg*. Retrieved from https://www.passiton.com/inspirational-quotes/8231-the-delicate-balance-of-mentoring-someone-is

19. Baranik, L. E., Roling, E. A., & Eby, L. T. (2010). Why does mentoring work? The role of perceived organizational support. *Journal of Vocational Behavior, 76*(3), 366–373. https://doi.org/10.1016/j.jvb.2009.07.004 (PMCID: PMC2855142)

20. Glaveski, S. (2019, April 17). *Leadership Lessons from Bill Campbell, the Trillion Dollar Coach*. Collective Campus. Retrieved from https://www.collectivecampus.io/blog/leadership-lessons-from-bill-campbell-the-trillion-dollar-coach

21. Sheikh, K. R. (2020, January 15). *Law Firms Can Do Better With Their Mentoring Programs*. Major, Lindsey & Africa. Retrieved from https://www.mlaglobal.com/en/insights/articles/law-firms-can-do-better-with-their-mentoring-programs